Christ and the Virgin

CHRIST
AND THE
VIRGIN

THE FORGOTTEN PURPOSE
OF CHRISTIANITY

Samael Aun Weor

GLORIAN

Christ and the Virgin
A Glorian Book

© 2013 Glorian Publishing

Print ISBN: 978-1-934206-90-4
Ebook ISBN: 978-1-934206-74-4

Originally published in Spanish as:
El Cristo Cósmico y la Semana Santa
El Libro de la Virgen del Carmen
Mensaje de Navidad 1961-1962

Glorian Publishing is a non-profit organization.
All proceeds go to further the distribution
of these books. For more information, visit
gnosticteachings.org.

v

Contents

Illustrations

The Cosmic Christ and the Holy Week

Before all, it is necessary to profoundly comprehend what in reality is the "Cosmic Christ."

In the name of truth, it is urgent to know that the Christ is not merely someone historical. People are used to thinking of Christ as a historical personage that existed 1,979 years ago. That concept is erroneous, because Christ is not of time. The Christ is timeless! The Christ unfolds Itself from instant to instant, moment to moment. Christ is the sacred fire, the cosmic, sacred fire.

If we were to strike a match, fire will germinate. Scientists say that fire is the result of combustion, but this is false. The fire that germinates from the match is contained within the match. Only when we strike the match do we free it from imprisonment, and the flame appears. We can say then that fire in itself is not the result of combustion, but rather, combustion is the result of the fire.

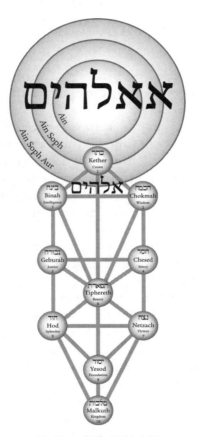

The Tree of Life (Kabbalah)

My dear brothers and sisters, it is important to know that what interests us most is the fire of the fire, the flame of the flame, the astral fire.

The hand that strikes the match so that the flame appears has fire, life, otherwise it would not be able to move.

After the match dies off, the flame continues to exist in the Fourth Vertical.

The scientists do not know what the fire is. They utilize it, but do not know it. Thus, my dear brothers and sisters, it is important for you to comprehend what the fire is.

The fire made its appearance before the dawn of creation vibrated intensely.

Remember, my dear brothers and sisters, that there are two Ones! The first One is Aelohim [אאלהים]! The second is Elohim [אלהים]! The first One is the unknown, the incognito, the divinity that cannot be painted, symbolized, or sculpted. The second One germinates from the first One, and is the Demiurge architect of the universe: the fire.

I wish you to understand that one is the fire that burns in the earth and the altar, and another is the fire of the spirit, like Aelohim or Elohim! Elohim is, therefore, the Demiurge, the Army of the Voice, the grand Word. Each one of the constructors of the universe is a living flame, living fire. It is written that God is a devouring fire.

The fire is the Christ, the Cosmic Christ. Elohim germinated from Aelohim. When Elohim unfolds, he endures as Two, to initiate cosmic manifestation into its wife, the Divine Mother. When the One unfolds into the Two, then emerges the Three, which is the fire. The beings of the fire fertilize the waters of existence, and then the Chaos converts itself into the "divine androgyne."

Thus it is important to comprehend that the Army of the Voice, the Army of the Word, is fire, and that living fire, that Philosophical Fire that fertilizes the chaotic matter, is the Cosmic Christ, the "Logos," the grand Word! But, in order for the Logos to come into manifestation, the One must unfold into the Two. That is to say: the Father unfolds into the Mother, and from the union of the two opposites is born the Three, the fire! That fire is the Logos, the Christ that in the dawn of any creation makes the existence of the universe possible.

It is important to understand better what Christ is, so we will not be content with merely remembering the historical account, because the Christ is a reality from instant to instant, moment to moment, second to second. He is the Creator.

The fire has the power to create atoms and disintegrate them, the ability to use the universal cosmic powers, etc. The fire has the power to unite all the atoms and create universes, or to disintegrate universes. The world is a fireball that either burns or goes out according to the laws.

Now I believe you are beginning to understand why we are interested in the subject of the astral fire, the Flame of the flame, the hidden, the esoteric aspect of the fire.

In reality, it is the fire that is Christic, that has the power to transform all that is, all that has been, and all that will be. Without "INRI," it would not be possible to Christify ourselves.

As I have said, the intimate Christ, the Cosmic Christ, has to take three steps from the bottom to top through the seven regions of the universe. I have also simply said that the Christ must take three

steps from bottom to top. Here is the
mystery of the three and seven steps of
Freemasonry. It is a true shame that the
Masonic brothers have forgotten all this.

In any case, the Christos, the Logos,
shines at the zenith of the spiritual midnight, and in the west and east. These
three points are repeated in all seven
regions.

The mystic who guides himself by the
star of the night, by the Spiritual Sun,
knows what those three steps mean in the
seven regions.

Let us also think of the Sun, the lightning, and the fire. Here are the three
lights, the three aspects of the Logos, in
the seven regions.

When the One unfolds into the Two,
the Third emerges; this is the fire, and it
creates and creates again. This One can
create with the power of the Word, the
Solar Word, Magic Word, or Word of the
Central Sun. Thus, the Logos is created.

By means of the fire, we can Christify
ourselves. It is vain for the Christ to be
born in Bethlehem if he is not born in our
hearts. Fruitless is his crucifixion, death,
and resurrection in the holy land if he is

not born, does not die, or resurrect in ourselves as well.

We need to incarnate the Cosmic
Christos, the spirit of fire, to make it flesh
in ourselves. As long as we stand idle,
we are dead to the things of the Spirit,
because it is the life, the Logos, the grand
Word... Heru-pa-kro-at!

He is Vishnu. The word Vishnu comes
from the root "vish," which means "to
penetrate." He penetrates everything that
is, has been, and will be. We need him to
penetrate us so that He can change us
radically. He who pretends to disintegrate
the ego with only the intellect marches
along in error.

Vishnu and Lakshmi, the Hindu depic-
tion of Elohim ("god and goddess")

Self-knowledge

Obviously, we need to know ourselves if we really want to Christify ourselves. If we want to know ourselves to achieve the Christification, we need to observe ourselves, to see ourselves. Only in this way is it possible for us to one day arrive at the disintegration of the ego.

The ego is the sum total of all our defects: anger, lust, greed, envy, pride, laziness, gluttony, etc. Even if we had a thousand tongues to speak, and a palate of steel, we would not be able to precisely articulate the number of all our defects.

As I have said, we need to observe ourselves to know ourselves. If we observe ourselves, we discover our psychological defects, and then we can work on them. When someone admits that he has a psychological defect, he begins to observe himself. This, in fact, converts him into a different being.

My dear Gnostic brothers and sisters, I want you to understand the necessity of learning to observe oneself, to see oneself; however, one must know how to observe, because there is one way—mechanical observation—and another: conscious observation.

Someone who hears of our teaching for the first time would say, "But what do I gain from observing myself? I have seen that I have anger, jealousy. So what?" Well, it is quite clear that this is mechanical observation! We need to observe the observed! This is conscious observation of ourselves.

Mechanical observation of ourselves cannot take us anywhere. It is absurd, unconscious, sterile. We need conscious self-observation in order to work on our defects.

If we feel anger in a given moment, let us observe the observed, the scene of anger. We must not put it off and do it later; let us do it now. When we observe the observed, what we see in ourselves, we will really know if it was anger or not, because it could have been a nervous syncope that we mistook for anger.

If, suddenly, we are invaded by jealousy, well, let us observe the observed. What was it that we observed? Maybe the woman was with another man! Or, if a woman, the man was with another woman! And we felt jealous. In any case, in a serene and profound meditation, let us observe the observed to know if, in reality, there was jealousy or not.

When we observe the observed by means of meditation and the obvious self-reflection, we therefore turn observation into consciousness. When we become conscious of such and such a psychological defect, we can work on it with the fire.

We would have to concentrate on Stella Maris, Tonantzin, Rhea, Martha, etc., who are derived from one part of our Being, and is the igneous serpent or our magical powers. The sacred cobra of ardent fire, with her flaming powers, can disintegrate the psychological defect, the psychic aggregate that we have consciously observed. It is obvious that at the same time the essence or fire embottled in the psychic aggregate that we disintegrate will shine, will be freed. And as we go on disintegrating the aggregates, the percentage of the essence, which is the Christic fire, will multiply. Finally, one day, the fire will shine fully inside ourselves, here and now.

We need the fire to seethe in us. Only the sacred name or INRI, put on the cross of the martyr of Calvary, can break the psychic aggregates. All those who do not take the fire into account pretend to eliminate all their aggregates, and march down a mistaken path. They are not only heading the wrong way, but also confuse others.

The Birth of Christ

It is said that Christ was born in the town of Bethlehem about 1,979 years ago. This is false, because the town of Bethlehem did not exist at that time. Bethlehem has a Chaldean root, ben, and ben is fire, the tower of fire of the Chaldeans. In our body, the head and neck are the tower because the rest of the body is the temple. He who has been able to bring up the fire in himself, he who has brought it up to his brain, up to the top, in fact, will be able to convert himself into the body of the "Christus," the fire, the spirit of the fire.

The primeval, original fire is able to totally Christify us. It is the fire, "Fohat," blazing within us that will transform us totally. Once the fire blazes in us, we will be transformed into totally different beings. We will become distinct beings. Then we will enjoy full illumination and

Christ is the blessed child that
must be born in each being.

cosmic powers. Thus, once understood, my brothers and sisters, we must work with the fire.

> *Whosoever knows, the word gives power. No one has uttered it; no one will utter it, except the one who has the Word incarnated.*

Christ, the spirit of fire, is not merely an historical personage. He is the Army of the Voice. He is the force that is beyond personality, ego, and individuality. He is a force like electricity and magnetism, a power, a great cosmic and universal manifestation. He is the cosmic fire that enters into the person who is adequately prepared, into the person who has that tower of Bethlehem ablaze. When Christ incarnates inside a person, she is radically transformed.

Christ is the blessed child that must be born in each being. Thus, as he was born in this universe millions of years ago to totally transform this solar system, he must be born in each one of us.

He was born in the stable of Bethlehem. That is to say, he is born among the animals of desire, among the psychological aggregates that he needs to eliminate. Only the fire can eliminate such aggregates. Thus, wherever these aggregates are, the fire arrives to destroy them, to reduce them to cosmic dust, and to free the essence. How can he free the soul if He does not enter profoundly into the human organism?

In the Orient, Christ is Vishnu, and I repeat, the word vish means "to penetrate." The fire, the Christ, the Logos, can penetrate profoundly into the human organism to burn the scum we have in ourselves. But we need to love the fire, to render cult to the flame.

The hour has come to understand that only "Fohat" can transform us radically. The Christ inside ourselves works to eliminate the roots of evil. INRI eliminates the psychological aggregates. This is formidable. It reduces them to ashes, but it is necessary to work with the fire.

This is why, in our works of concentration, we must invoke the igneous serpent of our magical powers, because only with the fire can we eliminate all the undesirable psychic elements that we carry within. The lunar coldness will never be able to eliminate the psychic aggregates. We need the flaming powers of the Logos. We need "INRI" to transform us.

The Seven Steps

My dear brothers and sisters, understand what the Holy Week is, and what the seven days of the Holy Week are.

In ancient times, everything was directed by the solar calendar: Moon, Mercury, Venus, Sun, Mars, Jupiter, and Saturn. The days were: Monday, Wednesday, Friday, Tuesday, Thursday, and Saturday. Unfortunately, this calendar was altered by fanatical medieval people.

The Holy Week is profoundly significant. Remember the seven and three steps of Freemasonry. The Christ must seethe first of all in our human body. Later on, the flame must be deposited in the profoundness of the soul, and at last, in the profoundness of the spirit. These three steps through the seven spheres are profoundly significant. Obviously, these three

The Order of the Seven

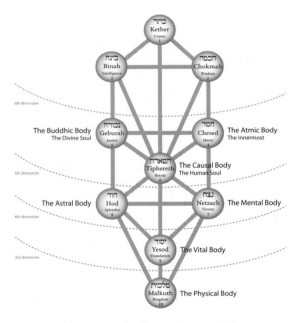

The first seven bodies on the Tree of Life

basic fundamental steps are found within the seven spheres of the world and the universe.

Unquestionably, the Holy Week has very deep esoteric roots, because the initiate must work on the lunar forces, and on the forces of Mercury, Venus, the Sun, Mars, Jupiter, and Saturn.

The Logos unfolds itself in the seven regions according to the seven planets of the solar system. The flame must appear in the physical body, must advance into the Vital body, must continue its passage through the Astral, must continue its journey through the world of the mind, must arrive at the sphere of Venus in the Causal world, must proceed through the Buddhic or Intuitive world, and at last, on the seventh day, it will arrive at the world of Atman, the world of the spirit. Then, the master will receive the baptism of the fire that will transform him radically.

Obviously, the whole cosmic drama as it is written in the four gospels must be lived inside ourselves, here and now. This is not something merely historical; it is something to be lived here and now!

The Three Traitors

The three traitors who crucified Christ, who gave him death, are inside us. The Masons know them. We Gnostics also know them: Judas, Pilate, and Caiaphas. Judas is the demon of desire that torments us. Pilate is the demon of the mind that has justifications for everything. Caiaphas is the demon of laziness that prostitutes the altar.

These are the traitors who crucified Christ for thirty coins of silver. The thirty coins of silver represent all the vices and passions of the world. They trade Christ for a few bottles at the bar. They trade Christ for the brothel of the adulterous bed. They trade Christ for money and riches, and for the sensual life. They sell Christ for thirty coins of silver.

Dear brothers and sisters, remember that a multitude of people asked for the crucifixion of the Lord. All that multitude yelled out, "Crucifixion! Crucifixion!" These are not the multitudes of 1,979 years ago. No! These people who demand the crucifixion of the Lord are inside us here and now. I repeat, here and now!

John 19:5

These are the psychic, inhuman aggregates that we carry in our interior. All are undesirable psychic elements that we carry inside, the red demons of "Seth," living personifications of all our psychological defects. They are the ones that cry, "Crucifixion! Crucifixion!" and the Lord is rendered to death. Who whipped Him? Are they not the same multitudes we carry in our interior? Who spit on Him? Are they not the same psychic aggregates that personify our defects? Who crowned Him with a crown of thorns? Are they not the same engenderers of the inferno that we have created?

The account of the Christic history is not of yesterday, but of today. It is the present, not merely the past, as the illustrious ignorants believe. Those who will understand, however, will work for Christification.

The Lord is elevated to Calvary, and on top of the majestic summits of Calvary will say, "He who believes in me shall never walk in darkness, but will have the light of life. I am the bread of life. I am the living bread. Whoever eats from my flesh and drinks from my blood shall have eternal life, and I shall raise him from the dead in the last day. Whoever eats from my flesh and my blood, I live in him and he in Me. The Lord bears no malice for anyone. Dear Father, in your hands I commend my spirit."

Once these grand words are pronounced, no other sounds can be heard but thunder and lightning amidst internal cataclysms. Once this opus of the spirit in the body is accomplished, the Christ or "Christos," the Christus, Vishnu, the one who penetrates, will be deposited in its mystical sepulcher.

I say unto you, in the name of truth and justice, that on the third day, after this third act, the initiate will be raised and resurrected to be transformed into a perfect being. He who achieves this will in fact become a God, terribly divine, beyond good and evil.

Thus the Christ, our Lord, the spirit of fire, descends and wants to enter each one of us, to transform us, save us, to eliminate all those psychic aggregates that we carry in our interior, to make out of us something distinct, to convert us into gods. We need to learn to see Christ not from a merely historical point of view, but as the fire, as a present reality, as "INRI."

The Apostles

It is said that he had twelve apostles. Those twelve apostles are inside us here and now.

There are twelve fundamental parts of our own Being, the twelve powers inside us, within our own profound interior Being.

There is Peter, who is in charge of the mysteries of sex.

There is John, who represents the Verb, the grand Word, Heru Pa Kro At!

There is also a Thomas, who teaches us to control the mind.

Inner Archetypes as Symbolized in Christianity

There is a Paul, who shows us the path of wisdom, philosophy, and Gnosis.

Inside ourselves we also find Judas. Not the Judas that sells Christ for thirty silver coins. No! It is a different Judas, a Judas who understands the ego profoundly, a Judas whose gospel takes us to the elimination of the self, the "I."

There is a Philip, who is capable of showing us how to travel through space out of the physical body.

There is an Andrew, who indicates with precise clarity that there are three factors of the revolution of consciousness:

- To be born—that is to say,
  how to create the superior
  existential bodies of the being
- To die—that is to say, how to
  eliminate the particular factors
  that specifically relate to us,
  and are in each one of us
- Sacrifice for humanity—Saint
  Andrews's cross, indicating the
  mixture of Sulfur and Mercury,
  so indispensable for the creation
  of the superior existential
  bodies of the being. This, by
  means of the accomplishment
  of the Being-Partkdolg-Duty,
  is significantly profound.

Within us there is a Matthew, a scientist like no other. He teaches us the pure science, unknown to the scientists that are in style nowadays, and tomorrow pass into history. Pure science is completely different! Only Matthew can instruct us in this.

Luke, with his Solar Gospel, is a prophet and shows us what life will be like in the Golden Age.

Each of the twelve is within us, because our Being has twelve fundamental parts, the twelve apostles, here and now. Thus,

whoever wishes to be a magician in the
true sense of the word [magician comes
from mag, "priest"], will have to learn to
relate to each part of the twelve parts of
the Being. This is only possible by burning the psychological aggregates with
"INRI." As long as the ego exists in us,
correct relations with each of the parts of
our Being will be impossible.

Erase from your mind the idea of the
twelve historical apostles. Search for
them inside of yourself. They are there!
Everything is inside us here and now!

The time has come for a more esoteric,
pure, real Christianity. It is time to leave
the merely historic account, and come to
the reality of the facts.

The cross is deeply significant. We
very well know that the vertical "phallus" inside the "uterus" forms the cross.
We will emphasize this in other words by
saying, "The lingam-yoni, connected cor-
rectly, form a cross."

With this cross, we need to advance
on the path that will conduct us to the
Golgotha of the Father. I invite all of you
to enter the path of Christification.

Do not forget that every time the lord of compassion comes to the world, he is hated by three types of people.

First, the elders, because they are people full of experience, say, "That man is crazy. Look what he is up to. Do not listen to what he says. He does not agree with us, with what we think. We have experience. This man destroys. He is dangerous."

Second, the scribes, that is to say, the intellectuals of all times reject him. Every time the lord of glory has come to the world, the intellectuals have been against him. They mortally hate him because he does not fit in with their theories. He signifies a danger to their system, to their sophisms, etc.

Third, the priests reject him, because all of them see him as a danger to their respective sects.

Then, in the name of truth, I tell you that the Christ is terribly revolutionary! Rebellious! He is the fire that comes to burn all the scummy rottenness that we carry inside. He is the fire that reduces to ashes all our prejudices, preconceptions, created interests, abominations, and even our personal experiences.

Do you believe, in fact, that the Christ can be accepted by so many millions of humans who live in the world? You are mistaken! Every time he comes to the world, the multitudes rise against him. This is the cruel reality of the facts.

I am talking of the Holy Week.

I say, in the name of truth, that only the "Fohat" seething in us can save us. No theory, nor any system, can take us to freedom. Those who want to pretend to eliminate the ego on the basis of pure reason, with the cold intellect, are being truly shallow! Habitual! Retardatory! They march on the path of great error.

This Babylon that we carry inside, this psychological city that we carry in our interior, the demons of lust, anger, greed, envy, pride, laziness, gluttony, etc, must be destroyed with the fire.

The Celestial Jerusalem

We need to raise the Celestial Jerusalem inside ourselves. Remember that the foundations of the Celestial Jerusalem are twelve, and on each one of them is written the name of an apostle. The name of the twelve apostles are on the twelve foundations. We must edify this Jerusalem inside ourselves. But it will only be possible on the day we with the fire destroy the Great Babylon, the mother of all fornications and abominations of the earth, the psychological city that we carry in our interior. When we accomplish this, we will edify the Celestial Jerusalem, here and now, inside us.

I repeat, the basis of the Celestial Jerusalem is the twelve apostles. I am not referring to those who lived 1,979 years ago as merely symbolic. No! I am talking about the twelve apostles that are inside us, the twelve conscious and independent parts of the Being. These are the foundations of the Jerusalem that we must edify inside ourselves.

The city of Jerusalem has twelve doors, and at each of the twelve doors is an Angel who represents one of the twelve inside us. The twelve doors are twelve precious pearls, twelve doors of liberty, twelve doors of light and splendor, and twelve cosmic powers. In the city, its streets, avenues, and plazas are of pure gold, the gold of the spirit that we must create in the forge of the Cyclops.

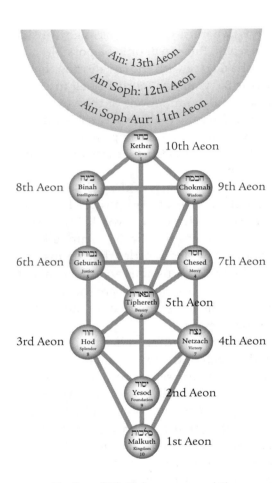

The Tree of Life. To learn more, read *The Gnostic Bible: The Pistis Sophia Unveiled*

The city has no necessity of external light, sun, or moon, because the Lord is its light, is the fire, and he will shine inside us.

The wall of the great city is 144 cubits. If we add those numbers in this way, one plus four plus four, we have nine, which is the Ninth Sphere, sex. Only through transmutation of the creative energy are we going to be able to make the fire shine within us.

The city is of twelve thousand stadia. It reminds us of the twelve works of Hercules, necessary to achieve the complete intimate realization of the Being. It reminds us of the twelve Aeons, and also of the twelve apostles.

In the center of this city is the Tree of Life, the Ten Sephiroth, the Hebrew Kabbalah: Kether, Chokmah, and Binah, with the sephirothic crown; Geburah, Tiphereth, Netzach, Hod, Yesod, and Malkuth, the seven regions of the universe. The Tree of Life allegorizes the twelve great cosmic regions. Happy is he who arrives at the Thirteenth Aeon, where Pistis Sophia should always be.

Inside the Celestial Jerusalem, we also find the twenty-four who prostrate to the earth, deposit the crowns at the feet of the Lamb, the immolated lamb of fire that shines in this universe from the aurora of creation, from the dawning of this universe. The twenty-four Elders are also twenty-four parts of our own Being.

Happy is the one who is nourished by the fruits of the Tree of Life, because she will be immortal! Happy is she who nourishes herself with each of those fruits. He who can really nourish himself with that current of life that comes from the Thirteenth Aeon to the human body will never know illness and will be immortal.

But in order to be able to nourish oneself with the Tree of Life, it is necessary above all to have eliminated all the psychic aggregates. Remember that the psychic aggregates are the living personifications of our errors that alter our Vital body, which damages the physical body. This is how disease and illnesses take place in us.

Who causes ulcers? Is it not anger?

Who causes cancer? Is it not lust?

Who causes paralysis? Is it not the materialistic, gross, selfish, and fatal life?

Diseases are caused by the psychic aggregates, or demons of Seth, living personifications of our errors. When all the red demons of Seth have been eliminated with the fire, when our own personality has been burned, then we can nourish ourselves with the Tree of Life. Life, descending from the Absolute through the thirteen Aeons, will penetrate into our body and make us immortal. Thus health is gained, and there will be no illness.

Useless are the scientists with all their curative methods. If they cure the patient, he will be sick again. It is true that the ego injects the venom of its morbidity and rottenness inside the organisms, and destroys them! Here is the origin of all diseases! People want a remedy to cure themselves, but as long as the ego is alive, people will always be sick.

The hour has come to understand that we need to burn down the Babylon inside us, and to edify Jerusalem.

The Celestial Jerusalem, seen from afar, is like jasper, like crystal. It is the Philosopher's Stone. Happy is he who obtains the Philosopher's Stone, because he will transform himself radically. He will have powers over the fire, over the air, over the waters, and over the earth!

We need a pure, esoteric Christianity, a living Christianity that can transform us radically. The Gnostic movement, the Gnostic Church, and our Gnostic anthropological studies will show humanity the path of liberation. But as we are now, with the ego alive, strong, and robust, we march on the path of error. We need to learn to love the fire, to work in reality with the mysteries of the fire!

Prologue

Ave Maria, Hail Mary

<small>In Latin:</small>

Ave Maria, gratia plena. Dominus tecum. Benedicta tu in mulieribus, et benedictus fructus ventris tui Iesus. Virginis Maria mater Dei, ora pro nobis cum peccatoribus ego, nunc, et in hora mortis vitium nostrae. Sela Fiat.

<small>In English:</small>

Hail Ram-IO, full of grace. Our Lord is with thee. Blessed art thou among women, and blessed is the fruit of thy womb, Yeshua. Virgin Ram-IO, Mother of God, pray for us with the sinning ego, now and at the hour of the death of our vices. Amen.

Chapter One

The Virgin of Carmel, the Mother of the Divine Redeemer of the World

Innumerable poets have sung praises to the greatest mother of all times. How can we define her? Neither the Madonna chiseled by Michelangelo nor the Madonna painted by Leonardo Da Vinci managed to faithfully portray the image of Virgin Mary.

Innumerable sculptures have tried to personify the Virgin of Carmel, but none of them accurately translated the physiognomy of this great daughter of the light.

When with the eyes of the soul we contemplate the ineffable figure of the divine mother, we do not see anything that resembles diamonds, rubies, and emeralds. Before the eyes of the soul, the purple silks that have wanted to wrap the memory of Mary, the divine mother of Jesus of Nazareth, completely disappear.

Indeed, Virgin Mary was not that worldly beauty painted in all the watercolors.

With the eyes of the spirit, we contemplate only a virgin brunette, burned by the desert sun.

Before our stunned spiritual eyes, the slender bodies and provocative feminine faces are blurred away, and in its place appears a simple young woman, small in stature, with a slim body, a small oval face, a blunt nose, a protruding upper lip, Gypsy eyes, and a wide forehead.

This humble woman wore a brown or Carmelite tunic with leather sandals.

She walked through the African deserts heading to the land of Egypt. She seemed like a prodigious woman, with her old and worn-out robe, her brown face soaked with copious sweat.

Mary is not that bluish, purple statue with diamonds that today adorns the Cathedral of Notre Dame de Paris.

Mary is not that statue whose ermine embedded fingers of pure gold gladden the processions of the parish house.

Mary is not that unforgettable beauty we contemplate on the sumptuous altars of our village churches, whose metal bells cheer the markets of our parish temples.

Before our spiritual senses, we see only a virgin brunette, burnt by the sun of the African desert.

Before the sight of the spirit, all fantasies completely disappear, and in its place appears a humble, prodigal woman of flesh and blood.

In childhood, Mary made vows of chastity in the temple of Jerusalem.

Mary was the daughter of Anna, who presented Mary to be received into the temple to take her vows. Thus, Mary was one of the vestals of the temple.

Mary was born from an aristocratic family. Before entering into the temple as

The Presentation to the Temple

a vestal, she had countless suitors, even a rich and handsome man who wanted to marry her. However, Mary did not accept him; her heart loved only God.

The first years of her life were surrounded by all sorts of comforts.

Traditions state that Mary made carpets for the temple of Jerusalem, and that those carpets were transformed into roses.

Mary knew the secret doctrine of the tribe of Levi. Mary was educated within the august shadows of the gates of Jerusalem, amidst the blooming foliage of oriental palms, under whose shadows rested the old camel riders of the desert.

Likewise, Mary was initiated into the mysteries of Egypt. She knew the wisdom of the Pharaohs, and drank from the goblet of ancient Christianity, calcined by the burning fire of the eastern lands.

The Catholic religion as we know it today did not loom upon the seven hills of the Augustan Rome of the Caesars; the ancient Essenians only knew the old Christian doctrine, the doctrine of the martyrs, that doctrine by which St. Stephen died a martyr.

That holy, Christic doctrine was kept in secrecy within the mysteries of Egypt, Troy, Rome, Carthage, Eleusis, etc.

The greatest task endowed upon Jesus Christ was to publicly represent that ancient doctrine on the roads of Jerusalem.

Thus, Mary, the virgin of Carmel, was the vestal chosen by divinity to be the mother of the divine redeemer of the world.

The Annunciation by Edward Burne-Jones (1879)

Chapter Two

Annunciation

"And in the sixth month, the angel Gabriel was sent from God unto a city of Galilee, named Nazareth, to a virgin espoused to a man whose name was Joseph, of the house of David; and the virgin's name was Mary. And the angel came in unto her, and said, Hail, thou that art highly favored, the Lord is with thee: blessed art thou among women. And when she saw him, she was troubled at his saying, and cast in her mind what manner of salutation this should be. And the angel said unto her, Fear not, Mary: for thou hast found favor with God. And, behold, thou shall conceive in thy womb, and bring forth a son, and shall call his name JESUS." – Luke 1:26-31

"Then said Mary unto the angel, how shall this be, seeing I know not a man?

"And the angel answered and said unto her, The Holy Ghost shall come upon thee, and the power of the Highest shall over-shadow thee: therefore also that holy thing which shall be born of thee shall be called the Son of God." - Luke 1:34, 35

"And Mary arose in those days, and went into the hill country with haste, into a city of Judah; and entered into the house of Zechariah, and saluted Elisabeth. And it came to pass, that, when Elisabeth heard the salutation of Mary, the babe leaped in her womb; and Elisabeth was filled with the Holy Ghost: And she spoke out with a loud voice, and said: Blessed art thou among women, and blessed is the fruit of thy womb.

"And whence is this to me that the mother of my Lord should come to me?

"For, lo, as soon as the voice of thy saluta-tion sounded in mine ears, the babe leaped in my womb for joy. And blessed is she that believed: for there shall be a performance of those things which were told her from the Lord. And Mary said, My soul doth magnify the Lord, And my spirit hath rejoiced in God my Savior. For he hath regarded the low estate of his handmaiden: for, behold, from henceforth all generations shall call me blessed. For he that is mighty hath done to me great things; and holy is his name. And his mercy is on them that fear him from generation to generation. He hath showed strength with his arm; he hath

scattered the proud in the imagination of
their hearts. He hath put down the mighty
from their seats, and exalted them of low
degree. He hath filled the hungry with good
things; and the rich he hath sent empty
away. He hath holpen his servant Israel,
in remembrance of his mercy; as he spoke
to our fathers, to Abraham, and to his seed
for ever. And Mary abode with her about
three months, and returned to her own
house." – Luke 1:39-56

In ancient times, the entire human spe-
cies conceived their children by the will
and grace of the Holy Spirit; back then,
there was no pain in childbirth.

The Holy Spirit sent his holy angels
to betroth men and women in the large
courtyards of the temples. Thus, the
sexual act was directed by angels, and this

The Angels Taught Humanity about Sex

was a sacrament that was only performed in the temples in order to engender bodies for the souls that needed to come into the world.

Back then, there was no pain in childbirth. Women gave birth to their children without pain, because they were conceived by the will and grace of the Holy Spirit. But, when humanity disobeyed the angels, humanity sinned against the Holy Spirit; thus the Holy Spirit said unto the woman, "I will greatly multiply thy sorrow and thy conception," and to the man, "In the sweat of thy face shall thou eat bread" to sustain your wife and your children. Adam represents all men of ancient times, and Eve all women of ancient times.

Mary had been following the path of chastity and holiness, and therefore she was surprised when the angel announced that she will conceive a son. By her example she taught the path of chastity.

In this day and age, marriage has become a license to fornicate. Men and women are multiplied merely by animal pleasure, not caring a whit about the Holy Spirit.

Any sexual union that is performed without the permission of the Holy

Spirit is fornication. The human beings
of this time do not want to understand
this, because they walked away from the
ancient doctrine known by the Virgin
Mary, mother of Jesus, and which was
preached by Christ on the unconquered
walls of Zion.

All the sages of the past engendered
their children by the will and grace of the
Holy Spirit. Zechariah was surprised when
the angel announced the birth of John the
Baptist. John was also engendered by the
will and grace of the Holy Spirit. An angel
announced to Zechariah that his already
old wife would conceive a son. Let us read
the following biblical verses.

> "And it came to pass, that while he ex-
> ecuted the priest's office before God in the
> order of his course, according to the custom
> of the priest's office, his lot was to burn
> incense when he went into the temple of
> the Lord. And the whole multitudes of the
> people were praying without at the time of
> incense. And there appeared unto him an
> angel of the Lord standing on the right side
> of the altar of incense.

> "And when Zechariah saw him, he was
> troubled, and fear fell upon him. But the

The Angel and Zechariah

*angel said unto him, Fear not, Zechariah:
for thy prayer is heard; and thy wife Elisabeth shall bear thee a son, and thou shall
call his name John. And thou shall have
joy and gladness; and many shall rejoice at
his birth. For he shall be great in the sight
of the Lord, and shall drink neither wine
nor strong drink; and he shall be filled with
the Holy Ghost, even from his mother's
womb." - Luke 1: 8-15*

All the great saints and sages of ancient
times were born by the will and grace of
the Holy Spirit.

Any upright and just marriage must
conceive by the will and grace of the Holy
Spirit.

Those spouses who want to be truly Christian must pray, asking the Holy Spirit for the annunciation. The angel of God will appear to the spouses in dreams, and will announce the day and time that they must perform the sexual connection.

Any child conceived in this way will be beautiful and pure from childbirth, because the child will be engendered by the will and grace of the Holy Spirit.

We must dominate carnal passion, and cultivate the purity and sanctity of marriage.

> *"Marriage is honorable in all, and the bed undefiled: but fornicators and adulterers God will judge."* - Hebrews 13:4

> *"Lest there be any fornicator, or profane person, as Esau, who for one morsel of meat sold his birthright."* - Hebrews 12:16

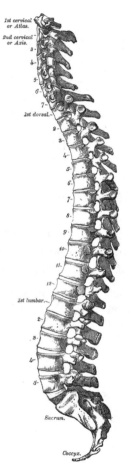

The spinal column has thirty-three vertabrae. It is the
rod of Aaron, the staff of the priest, the rod of Joseph.

Chapter Three

Conception

In the temple of Jerusalem, there were
33 male priests of the tribe of Levi.

Jesus of Nazareth's father Joseph
was one of 33 elders of the temple of
Solomon.

After the annunciation, the high priest
ordered all 33 priests of the temple to
place their rods behind the altar. They
were told that the one whose branch blos-
somed was destined to be the husband of
Mary. Thus, all the priests, one by one, in
successive order, placed their rods behind
the altar. The last one commanded to
place his rod was the priest Joseph, who
resisted the command of the high priest,
alleging his old age. However, he had to
obey the command, and placed his rod
behind the altar.

Early in the morning the next day, all
the priests went to the altar to collect
their rods, and to their great surprise they
found the rod of Joseph completely blos-
somed.

Flowering of Joseph's Rod

Thus, this is how Joseph was appointed to be the husband of Mary.

Thereafter, the virgin of Carmel was taken out of the temple and into the house of an honorable citizen of Jerusalem to await for the hour of conception.

The Angel Gabriel chose the day and hour so that the spouses could perform the sexual act as a sacrifice on the altar of marriage, to give a body to the divine redeemer of the world.

Mary was a virgin before childbirth, during childbirth, and after childbirth, because she was virginal in her soul, and because her conception was verified by the will and grace of the Holy Spirit.

When an angel commands the sexual act, it engenders children by the will and grace of the Holy Spirit.

The sexual act is pure for those who are pure, and impure for those who are impure.

When we look with angel eyes at the sexual act, it is angelic. However, when we look at it with malignant eyes, it is demonic.

The sexual act is holy when it is performed under the command of an angel. Yet, the sexual act is Satanic when it is performed under the command of the devil.

Mary did not have pain in childbirth, because her son was conceived by the will and grace of the Holy Spirit. So, if all the spouses of the world imitated Mary and Joseph, they would conceive their children by the will and grace of the Holy Spirit, by not fornicating. This is the wonderful key that allows the birth of smart children filled with beauty.

What is important is to know how to abstain, and pray daily to the Holy Spirit and his holy angel Gabriel, so that in dreams he can make us partakers of the annunciation. Then, in dreams the angel of the Lord will reveal the day and the hour in which the spouses may perform the sacred act of fertilization.

By means of this conception of the Holy Spirit, each home will become a paradise, and amorous disappointments will disappear, and there will be happiness.

The prayer to the Angel Gabriel must be performed as follows:

> *"Oh Iod-Havah Zabaoth, if thou wilt indeed look on the affliction of thine handmaid, and remember me, and not forget thine handmaid, but wilt give unto thine handmaid a man child, then I will give him unto Iod-Havah all the days of his life, and there shall no razor come upon his head."* – 1 Samuel 1:11

Chapter Four
The Mountain

We are souls that have a body. Thus, the body is nothing but a vesture for the soul.

The body does not think; thought is elaborated by the thinking soul. The body does not love; love is experienced by the soul. The body does not desire; desire is a craving of the animal soul. The body is nothing but a vesture for the soul.

During the hours of sleep, the soul leaves the body and visits all of those places that are familiar to it.

During the hours of sleep, the soul wanders through the sacred mountain that the saints of the Gospels speak about.

The Bible speaks about the mountain in the following verses.

> *"And it came to pass about an eight days after these sayings, he took Peter and John and James, and went up into a mountain to pray. And as he prayed, the fashion of his countenance was altered, and his raiment was white and glistering. And, behold,*

The Transfiguration

*there talked with him two men, which were
Moses and Elias: Who appeared in glory,
and spoke of his decease which he should
accomplish at Jerusalem. But Peter and
they that were with him were heavy with
sleep: and when they were awake, they saw
his glory, and the two men that stood with
him. And it came to pass, as they departed
from him, Peter said unto Jesus, Master, it
is good for us to be here: and let us make
three tabernacles; one for thee, and one*

*for Moses, and one for Elias: not knowing
what he said. While he thus spoke, there
came a cloud, and overshadowed them:
and they feared as they entered into the
cloud. And there came a voice out of the
cloud, saying, This is my beloved Son: hear
him. And when the voice was past, Jesus
was found alone. And they kept it close,
and told no man in those days any of those
things which they had seen. And it came to
pass, that on the next day, when they were
come down from the hill, much people met
him." – Luke 9:28-37*

The mountain that the Gospels talk
about is outer space.

During the hours of sleep, all souls go
up into the mountain, and wandering,
visit different places; they go where their
heart takes them.

During dreams, our souls converse with
distant beings, converse with other souls,
and can converse with the angels.

When it is stated that Christ, Peter,
John, and James went up into a mountain
to pray, and that Christ is transfigured in
the presence of them, we have to understand that their bodies of flesh and bones
slept, while their souls prayed outside
their bodies, in the mountain.

Every human being can visit the mountain at will. What is important is to comprehend that we are souls that have bodies, and that we can enter and leave the body at will.

Every Christian can learn to leave their body at will.

The clue is the following:

The person must lie in bed. When feeling as if already dozing, the person must placidly get up from bed, being careful of not awakening from sleep.

Thereafter, they will leave their room and perform a small jump with the intention of floating, and thus, flying, each one can go where their heart takes them. Any mother may visit her distant son, see him, and talk with him. The husband may visit his distant wife, see her, and she in turn may do the same.

This is not a mental practice. It is not a mental issue. When we state that the Christian must placidly rise from bed, this must be done as it is described, yet taking care of the sleepy state, because the power to enter "the mountain" is in the sleepy state.

What is important is to abandon laziness, and get up from the bed at the moment of dozing.

In the mountain, any soul can converse with the virgin of Carmel, and with the beloved son of her womb.

The most holy virgin of Carmel weeps for all women, and cares for all humans.

In the mountain, the virgin of Carmel is dressed in her Carmelite tunic.

She bears a Carmelite and brown mantle over her head, she carries a scapular in her hands, and a crown is wound upon her head.

This is the brunette virgin, the virgin of the mountain.

The Liberated Soul

Chapter Five

Discernment

In our former chapter, we stated that when the body sleeps, the soul roams about in the sacred mountain.

During the hours of sleep, the soul is occupied in the same exchanges and activities as the day.

When outside their bodies, merchants buy and sell in their stores, without realizing that they are outside their body.

During the hours of sleep, we see the souls of seamstresses, mechanics, shopkeepers, street vendors, etc., dedicated to the same jobs and necessities as the day. Those souls are asleep; they are convinced, they are sure, that they are within their bodies of flesh and bones. When someone tells them that they are outside their body, they do not believe it, and scoff at it.

If those souls realized they are outside their body, they could then transport themselves to any corner of the world in the blink of an eye.

Thus, the wife who suffers for the absent man she loves; the girlfriend who is suffering for her beloved boyfriend can visit him without being seen. The mother whose son is absent can visit her son, and know about his life.

What is important is to know the clue, the secret, in order to realize that one is outside the physical body. That clue is discernment.

During the day we must ask ourselves the following question: "Am I in the body? Am I out of the body?" Then jump; make a small jump with the intention of floating in the air. If one floats, it is because one is outside the body. Then, while hovering in the air, one goes to where ones heart wishes.

This question must be asked while in the presence of any curious thing. Let us suppose that one is walking down the street and meets a friend who has not bern seen for a long time; then, ask oneself the question: "Am I in the body or outside the body?" Then one performs a small jump with the intention of floating, and if one floats, it is because one's body is asleep in the bed, and one is outside of it. Then one goes to where one's heart takes it, towards the distant absent son, towards one's beloved relative.

So, one must question oneself during the day, while in the presence of any curious thing: a uproar, a rare item, an encounter with a deceased one, an encounter with a distant friend; to that end, in the presence of any little insignificant detail.

The clue of discernment must be practiced during the day, at every step, at every moment, so that it will be recorded very well in our soul, and thus be repeated when acting during sleep.

Everything that one consistently does during the day one is routinely doing during sleep, thus, if this practice is consistently done during the day, then during the night, during the hours of sleep, when as a soul one is out of the body, one will repeatedly do it.

Then in the moment of asking: "Am I in the body or outside the body?" One will execute the little jump exactly as one has done it during the day, thus ones Consciousness will awaken and will float in space; then one can visit distant relatives, the absent son, the mother of whom one has no news, etc.

Understand, during the hours of sleep the soul is outside the body; thus, in order to be able to visit any far place, what is important is to realize that one as a soul is outside of the body. So, this is the key of discernment.

Now, if when outside the body we pure-heartedly invoke the virgin of Carmel, then the divine mother of the Nazarene will answer our call and we will converse with her. And if when outside the body we invoke the Angel Gabriel, asking for the Annunciation, then he will tell the wife and the husband on which day and hour they can join their bodies. So, in this way women can conceive children by the will and grace of the Holy Spirit; in other words, by command of the Holy Spirit.

During sleep, souls can converse with angels. Thus, during sleep every man, every woman, every child, every elder, can converse with angels.

Outside the body, we can invoke the angels, and they will attend our call in order to teach us the word of God.

Chapter Six
Miracles of the
Virgin of Carmel

All of us who know the mountain know that the Virgin of Carmel is a tireless worker.

Often a devotee is cured of some incurable disease, and then, filled with admiration, exclaims, "A miracle done by the Virgin of Carmel!"

What the devotee ignores is that the Virgin of Carmel has had to work intensely in order to be able to heal the sick body.

On other occasions, a devotee has been saved from dying tragically, thus, full of admiration, he exclaims, "A miracle!" Yet the devotee ignores the supreme effort, the enormous sacrifice, the magnitude of work that the Virgin of Carmel had to perform.

We are going to narrate some miracles of the Virgin of Carmel:

1 By imploring the Virgin of Carmel, Alfredo Bello was saved from being drowned in a schooner. Alfredo Bello was sailing near the Panama Canal toward the

city of Barranquilla, when the schooner
broke. The ship sank within the raging
waves of the sea. Nothing was visible but
sky and water, not even a ray of hope.
Thus, Alfredo Bello grabbed a miserable
plank, and implored the Virgin of Carmel.
Thus, in time he received assistance; this
is how the man was saved. Thus, full
of admiration, exclaimed, "A miracle!"
Nonetheless, the man ignored the tremendous effort that the Virgin of Carmel had
had to do in order to save him.

2 José Prudencio Aguilar, a distinguished and exclusive gentleman of
Riohacha, was sailing a schooner in the
raging waves of the Atlantic ocean, when
it was suddenly hit by a terrifying hur-
ricane that stirred the raging waves of the
sea. That schooner was on the verge of
sinking into the depths of the ocean. The
man cried to the Virgin of Carmel, and
she worked very hard in order to save him
from disaster. "A miracle!" exclaimed the
man.

3 By invoking the Virgin of Carmel,
the lady Esther Lozano gave birth to
a beautiful girl without feeling any pain
in childbirth. "A miracle!" exclaimed the
lady, without realizing the enormous sci-

entific work that the Virgin of Carmel had to make in order to assist her. Gratefully, the lady baptized her daughter with the name of the Virgin of Carmel.

4 In the year 1940, sailing in a boat of Tacamocho Gamarra, in the moment she was bending to take a bucket of water, the lady Emilia Hernández fell into the water. She was in the raging waves of the Magdalena river for four hours, and grabbed an insignificant branch, yet she was saved from the claws of death by invoking the Virgin of Carmel. The name of the boat was "Manzanares." The Virgin of Carmel had to fight a lot in order to save the lady.

5 A sailor belonging to a distinguished family of Samaria had an accident in the sea, and lasted several hours in the water. He was rescued and became responsive again, and everyone exclaimed, "A miracle of the Virgin of Carmel!"

6 On one occasion a man that climbed a hill of Tolima was attacked by a vicious dog. In the darkness of the night, the animal howled. The frightened man invoked the Virgin of Carmel, and the beast fled scared. There is no doubt that

this animal was a tenebrous creature from the abyss.

7 And what we would say about the girl who was saved after the plane she was traveling in crashed? The aircraft transported a large number of refugee children from Germany to the United States, where it crashed. All of the children perished, but it remains unexplained how and in what way a completely healthy baby girl without a single scratch was found some distance from the plane. The Virgin of the Carmel did that wonderful work, that formidable miracle. We accept that by the law of destiny the girl should not have died just yet, but inevitably an intervention was needed, and it was precisely that of the Virgin of Carmel.

Chapter Seven
Nature

Nature is always a virgin mother. Nature is always a virgin, and always a mother. Nature is an austere and kind mother.

The consciousness of nature teaches the shy little bird to build its nest. The consciousness of nature beats in the heart of the tree, in the heart of the timid worm that crawls on the ground, in the heart of the eagle that haughtily flaps its intrepid wings above the gigantic masses of granite, which project their towering battlements into the blue of the sky. The consciousness of nature teaches the child to find his mother's breast, and teaches the birds to lift in flight. The consciousness of nature gives shape to all things, organizes the petals of the flowers that imbue the air with perfume, and order the movement of the stars amidst the magnificent orchestration of infinity.

Nature is an austere and loving mother. When we enter the mountain, we see her within her magnificent temple, with a golden crown and glittering white robe, governing the battling elements.

When humanity bothers her too much, she does what all mothers do with their children: she gives them toys to play with, she places in the mind of inventors the radio, airplane, automobile, etc., so that her children can have fun while they become mature to study the wisdom of God.

All the innocent angels of the earth, water, fire, and air obey the blessed goddess of the world.

Mary, Adonia, Insobertha, Isis, Astarte, have always symbolized the heavenly virgin nature.

Nature is a great workshop where God works.

Nature is the temple of the virgin mother of the world.

Chapter Eight

The Gnostic Church

Now we are going to teach the devotees of the Virgin of Carmel the path of true Christianity.

Let us study the third chapter of the first Epistle of the Apostle Paul to Timothy; let us read:

> *"This is a true saying, If a man desire the office of a bishop, he desires a good work.*

> *"A bishop then must be blameless, the husband of one wife, vigilant, sober, of good behavior, given to hospitality, apt to teach; not given to wine, no striker, not greedy of filthy lucre; but patient, not a brawler, not covetous; one that rules well his own house, having his children in subjection with all gravity;*

> *"(For if a man know not how to rule his own house, how shall he take care of the church of God?)*

> *"Not a novice, lest being lifted up with pride he fall into the condemnation of the devil.*

"Moreover he must have a good report of them which are without; lest he fall into reproach and the snare of the devil.

"Likewise must the deacons be grave, not double tongued, not given to much wine, not greedy of filthy lucre; holding the mystery of the faith in a pure conscience.

"And let these also first be proved; then let them use the office of a deacon, being found blameless.

"Even so must their wives be grave, not slanderers, sober, faithful in all things.

"Let the deacons be the husbands of one wife, ruling their children and their own houses well.

"For they that have used the office of a deacon well purchase to themselves a good degree, and great boldness in the faith which is in Christ Jesus.

"These things write I unto thee, hoping to come unto thee shortly:

"But if I tarry long, that thou may know how thou ought to behave thyself in the house of God, which is the church of the living God, the pillar and ground of the truth.

"And without controversy great is the mystery of godliness: God was manifest in the flesh, justified in the Spirit, seen of angels, preached unto the Gentiles, believed on in the world, received up into glory."

This is the Epistle of Paul the Apostle to Saint Timothy, pious and God-fearing man.

This is the holy doctrine of Saint Augustine, Saint Thomas, Clement of Alexandria, Hippolytus, Epiphanius, Carpocrates, who founded several monasteries in Spain, Tertullian, Saint Ambrose, Saint Stephen who died a martyr, Saint Justinian, etc.

This is the ancient doctrine that Christ taught in secret to his 70 disciples, and the reason why the saints were persecuted in Jerusalem.

This is the doctrine of the great princes of the Church. This is the doctrine of the Gnostics , which belonged to the primeval Gnostic Catholic Church dignitaries.

This is the ancient Christianity that Paul preached in Rome when he arrived loaded with chains. This is Christianity, which the Virgin of Carmel studied under the augustan shadows of the temple of Jerusalem.

Let us look at some other teachings of the Apostle Paul.

"Follow after charity, and desire spiritual gifts, but rather that ye may prophesy.

"For he that speaks in an unknown tongue speaks not unto men, but unto God: for no man understands him; howbeit in the spirit he speaks mysteries.

"But he that prophesies speaks unto men to edification, and exhortation, and comfort.

"He that speaks in an unknown tongue edifies himself; but he that prophesies edifies the church.

"I would that ye all spoke with tongues, but rather that ye prophesied: for greater is he that prophesies than he that speaks with tongues, except he interpret, that the church may receive edifying.

"Now, brethren, if I come unto you speaking with tongues, what shall I profit you, except I shall speak to you either by revelation, or by knowledge, or by prophesying, or by doctrine?" - 1 Corinthians 14:1-6

Thus, Saint Paul of Tarsus advises to all the good Christians to practice charity, to seek spiritual gifts, and especially that they prophesize.

"If any man speaks in an unknown tongue, let it be by two, or at the most by three, and that by course; and let one interpret.

"But if there be no interpreter, let him keep silence in the church; and let him speak to himself, and to God.

"Let the prophets speak two or three, and let the other judge.

"If any thing be revealed to another that sitteth by, let the first hold his peace.

"For ye may all prophesy one by one, that all may learn, and all may be comforted.

"And the spirits of the prophets are subject to the prophets.

"For God is not the author of confusion, but of peace, as in all churches of the saints.

"Let your women keep silence in the churches: for it is not permitted unto them to speak; but they are commanded to be under obedience, as also saith the law.

"And if they will learn any thing, let them ask their husbands at home: for it is a shame for women to speak in the church.

"What? came the word of God out from you? or came it unto you only?

> "If any man think himself to be a prophet,
> or spiritual, let him acknowledge that the
> things that I write unto you are the com-
> mandments of the Lord.

> "But if any man be ignorant, let him be
> ignorant.

> "Wherefore, brethren, covet to prophesy,
> and forbid not to speak with tongues.

> "Let all things be done decently and in
> order." - 1 Corinthians 14:27-40

Every good Christian can receive the
Holy Spirit and prophesize. Nevertheless,
whosoever wants to become a prophet
must be completely chaste and holy.

The Church of our Lord Jesus Christ
is not of this world; he himself said it,
"My kingdom is not of this world." In
the mountain of the living God, there is a
church, invisible to the eyes of the flesh,
but visible to the eyes of the soul and
the spirit. That is the primeval Gnostic
Church, to which Christ and the prophets
belong.

That church has its bishops, archbish-
ops, deacons, subdeacons, and priests who
officiate at the altar of the living God.
The patriarch of that invisible church is
Jesus Christ.

All Christians can go in soul and spirit to that church.

In chapters four and five of this book we teach the secret to consciously exit the body and thus visit any distant land on the Earth.

All humans can also visit the Gnostic Church during sleep. There in that holy church, we see the Virgin of Carmel together with her holy angels.

All the great saints of the church of God visit the Gnostic Church. Fridays and Sundays in the aurora there are masses and communions. By following the teachings given in chapters four and five of this book, all Christians can attend these masses and receive the communion of bread and wine.

In that church, all the devotees will be taught to prophesize.

In the Gnostic Church, we see Christ seated on his throne, and all the Gnostics can converse with him personally.

All the sufferings of Mary occurred when she married Joseph, the priest.

Mary was initiated in the mysteries of Egypt.

In the Gnostic Church, Christians learn how to prophesize.

The first miracle of Jesus was at a wedding.

What is important is to follow the path of perfect sanctity and chastity.

In our books entitled "The Perfect Matrimony" and "The Revolution of Beelzebub," we thoroughly study the great mysteries of sex. In those books, we teach the greatest secrets of the universe.

May peace be to all human beings.

The Avatar of Synthesis

Beloved:

It is said that there are seven great religions and five thousand sects. We the Gnostics affirm that there is only one great religion, and that is the TRUTH.

We firmly believe that only he who lives the Truth is profoundly religious.

The Truth wants to know itself in each man. Jesus of Nazareth is a living embodiment of the TRUTH. Jesus incarnated the TRUTH. Whoever incarnates the TRUTH becomes free.

Those who incarnated the Truth founded the great religions and the great mystery schools.

Buddha, Hermes, Krishna, Quetzalcoatl, etc. incarnated the Truth, and all those who dissolve the I and erect the columns of the temple upon the living rock incarnate the Truth.

There is no higher religion than the Truth.

We should distinguish between religious forms and religious principles. It is necessary to know that the principles are living cosmic formulae.

Religious forms are the different systems of teaching those principles.

The great infinite universal cosmic religion assumes distinct forms according to the needs of each race and era.

In this manner, religious forms have succeeded one another throughout millions of years. The successive string of the all religions that have existed in the world always reveals the same immutable principles of the Truth.

Religion is an inherent property of life, as humidity is of water.

A man could belong to no religion and yet be profoundly religious.

Every person who is capable of experiencing the Truth is profoundly religious, even if he does not belong to any religion. Religion is the intimate relationship of the mind with the Truth. Only the religious man is truly revolutionary.

Some philosophers say that religions have failed. We assure you that every religion has fulfilled its historic mission. Buddhism fulfilled its mission with the birth of merely one living Buddha. One Christified person justifies the existence of Christianity. One Imam well justifies the existence of the religion of Mohammed.

All the great religions of the world have achieved their objectives through men who obtained their "religare"—in other words, who incarnated the Truth.

Really, many are called, but few are chosen. This law has already been fulfilled in all the religions.

There is no basis for assuring that religions failed in their mission to "religare" [reunite] man with the Truth. In all religions are perfect ones who succeeded in reuniting the soul or consciousness with God.

There is no justification for religious wars, because all religions teach the same principles. The witch in mid-Africa and the archbishop in the Metropolitan Cathedral of Rome or London are based on the same marvelous force of the cosmic religion. The principles are the same. The only thing that varies is the religious form. Therefore, fratricidal struggle among diverse religions is absurd.

The cosmic religion vibrates in each atom of the cosmos, because it palpitates in the heart of the suns, in the heart of man, and in that of the ant.

The Mechanical Evolution of Nature

When death arrives, there is something that continues. That something is the I (legion of elementary demons), memory, which in turn is conditioned mind.

We assure you that the I is a bunch of memories. We affirm that the I is time. We assure you that the I returns to satisfy dissatisfied desires. We affirm that the I (legion of demons) never purifies or perfects itself.

We need to die from instant to instant. Only with the death of the I does one enter Nirvana. Only with the death of the I is the Christ born in the divine dwelling of the Soul.

The internal Christ does not evolve, because he is perfect. The internal Christ is the Truth that wants to know itself in each man.

Mechanical evolution of nature exists, but cannot lead to perfection. We need a tremendous revolution of our consciousness. When the I is dissolved, there is a revolution of our consciousness.

The Synthesis of Gnosis

The synthesis of the Universal Christian Gnostic Movement is summed up into two principles: dissolve the I, and erect the columns of the temple of the living God.

The Seven Columns of the Temple of Wisdom

The temple of wisdom has seven columns, and the word INRI is written in characters of fire on each of the seven columns. Only with INRI can we erect the temple for the internal Christ. The seven columns are erected upon the Philosopher's Stone (sex).

The Menorah, symbol of the soul, which is based on the sephirah Yesod ("foundation"), the sexual organs.

Jesus of Nazareth

Jesus was not the first one who incarnated the Truth, and neither shall he be the last.

The Hierophant Jesus has the same attributes of Zeus, Jupiter, Apollo, Krishna, Quetzalcoatl, and like them, also had his immaculate conception in the womb of a virgin.

Mythology says that Jesus was born on the 25th of December (the birth date of the God Mithra) in the town of Bethlehem, a town that did not exist in those times.

The name Bethlehem is derived from the word Bel or Belen, the Sun God of the Babylonians and Germans. The term Bethlehem indicates the Cosmic Christ, the Sun God, the Solar Logos.

The poor and unknown Hebrew woman Miriam (Mary) received the same attributes and cosmic powers of the goddesses ISIS, Juno, Demeter, Ceres, Vesta, Maia, Adonia, Insoberta, Rhea, Cybele, etc.

Mary is fecundated by the Holy Spirit. The latter, in the form of a dove, fecundates Mary's womb. The dove is a phallic symbol; let us remember Peristera, a nymph in the court of Venus, transformed by love into a dove.

The womb of the Virgin Mother is fecundated only with Sexual Magic, so that the Child God may be born in the manger of the world.

In the life of Jesus, Iesus, Zeus, Jupiter, Nazarenus, surges a passionate woman named Mary Magdalene, and she rapidly occupies the place of Salambo, Matra, Ishtar, Astarte, Aphrodite, and Venus.

The entire life of Jesus, Iesus, Zeus, and Jupiter, is similar to the life of Krishna in India, to that of the other Christified Beings of the world. That is why the Gospel of Jesus is similar to that of Krishna.

There are no differences in hierarchy in the Cosmic Christ. We are all ONE in the world of the Truth. However, it is good to clarify that the Buddha Jesus is the most exalted Master of the universe. Buddha is the Realized Spirit in every Perfect Man.

Christ is the Truth.

The birth of Jesus the Christ—and his life, passion, death, and resurrection—should be lived by everyone who Christifies himself.

The only true image of our Lord Jesus Christ

*Taken from an emerald engraving ordered by Tiberius,
Roman Emperor. It comes from the treasury of
Constantinople and it was given to Pope Innocent
VIII by the Sultan of Turkey in payment for the res-
cue of his brother, held captive by the Christians.
This picture was taken directly from the price-
less emerald belonging to the Vatican Treasury.*

The Nicene Council

At the Nicene Council celebrated 325
A.D., two things were recognized: first,
a man who incarnated the Truth; second, the doctrine, the primitive Gnostic
Christian esotericism.

Jesus is the Christ because he incarnated the Christ. Jesus, Iesus, Zeus, Jupiter is
the new Christ-man who in fact initiated
a new era.

The Nicene Council was a necessity of
the time because the ancient religious
form of Roman Paganism had entered
into total degeneration and death. It was

The Nicene Council

becoming necessary to dress the universal cosmic principles of the cosmic religion with a new religious form. The Nicene Council was definitive: to initiate a new era, the religious principles were dressed in new clothes, and that is how Christianity was born.

The Christian Form

The Titan Demi-gods, goddesses, sylphids, cyclops, and messengers of the Gods were rebaptized with the names Angels, Archangels, Seraphims, Powers, Virtues, Thrones, etc.

The terrible Roman Avernus, symbol of the atomic infernos of man and nature, was rebaptized with the name Hell.

Olympus, dwelling place of the gods, was converted into the Christian Heaven. Every religion has its Heaven. Let us remember the Chinese Heaven, the Heavens of the Gennans, of the Scandinavians, of the Japanese, etc. Every religious Heaven represents the Superior Worlds studied by occultism.

Thus, under the disguise of the new Christian man, the clerical organization was formed anew with the same attributes, ceremonies, miters, and liturgies of Paganism.

The religious form of Paganism degenerated and died, but its principles continued in Christianity. During the latter times of Paganism, people laughed at the mitered, and the priests wandered on the streets as vagabonds, or became puppeteers, importunates; many passed themselves off as fortune tellers and were stoned on the streets by the multitudes. That is the end of every religious form. When the multitudes do not respect a religious form, it disappears.

The Cult to Fire

The God Khristus (Christ) comes from very ancient cults to the god of fire. The interlaced P and the X represent the P (pyre) and the X (cross). Hence, this is the hieroglyph to produce the fire. That cult reappeared with the famous Nicene Council. It is necessary to produce the fire, to work with the sacred fire to achieve Christification. (The Arcanum A.Z.F. is the key).

Chi Rho

Priests and Nuns

The priests of Paganism—denominated augur, druid, flamen, hierophant, dionysus and sacrificator—were later converted into priests, clergymen, pastors, prelates, pope, anointed, abbot, theologian, etc.

The priestesses of the ancient mysteries with whom the initiates practiced Sexual Magic were Christianized with the different names of the nun orders. The

Vestals of the temple

sybil, vestal, druidess, popess, deacon-
ess, menade, pythoness, etc., were transformed into novice, postulant, sister or
nun, abbess, canoness, prelate, superior,
reverend. It is a pity that these religious
women have forgotten or lost the key of
Sexual Magic.

If the priests of Christianity had not
departed from primeval Gnosis, the nuns
would have been their priestesses, and
would have then practiced the Arcanum
A.Z.F. with them, and in this way,
Christianity would have been very different.

Phallic Origin

All religions have a SEXUAL origin. Sexual Magic was practiced in all the religions. There is phallicism in all cults. In all the great religions were priestesses of love, sacred vestals, women who only served for Sexual Magic. The great celibate initiates practiced Sexual Magic with those nuns or priestesses of the temples. That is how they realized themselves in depth. The Hierophant Jesus also practiced Sexual Magic with a priestess of the pyramid of Kephren.

Jesus seated on the Foundation Stone

There were mystery schools with phallic worship in all civilizations. Without this worship, no one can achieve the Christmas of the heart.

In Asia and Africa, it is still easy to find the current of adoration to the lingam, yoni, and pudenda, and to the seed also.

Among many others, the following divinities were consecrated to the phallic worship: Siva, Agni, Shakti, in India; Legba in Africa; Venus, Bacchus, Priapus, and Dionysus in Greece and Rome; also the Jews had phallic idols, and forests consecrated to this worship, without which Christification is impossible.

In Greece and Rome, in the temples of Venus, Vesta, Aphrodite, and Isis, the priestesses of love marvelously exercised their sexual priesthood.

Types of Crosses

1. St. Anthony's
2. Latin
3. St. Andrew's
4. Greek
5. Monogrammatic
6. Monogrammatic
7. Swastika
8. Egyptian or Ankh
9. Patriarchal
10. Maltese

The nuns of Pacadoccia, Antioch, Cyprus, and Byblos celebrated gigantic processions majestically carrying an enormous phallus made of sacred wood; they knew that the secret key to Christification is in the union of the phallus and the uterus.

In reality, all that comes to life has its germ, likewise it is true that the Internal Master is not born from nothing. The Internal Master is born from its living germ, which is deposited in the seminal system, in sanctity, in the Christ, and the synthesis of all religions is found in Sexual Magic. Every religion of the world has its esotericism, the Christ, Sexual Magic, and sanctity.

The universal Gnostic Christian Movement teaches the doctrine of the synthesis.

The Christ in Substance

Christ is not a human nor divine individual. Christ is a Cosmic substance, latent in each atom of the infinite. The Christ substance is the substance of the Truth. Christ is the Truth and life.

When a man assimilates the Christ substance physically, psychically, and spiritually, he becomes Christified; he is transformed into Christ; he is converted into the living Christ. We need to form Christ within us. It is urgent to incarnate the Truth.

Christified Beings

Among the Chinese, Christ is Fu-Xi. The Chinese Christ is miraculously born by the work and grace of the Holy Spirit.

> *"Walking by the river bank, a virgin named Hoa-Se placed her foot on the footprint of the Great Man; immediately she was moved, seeing herself surrounded by a marvelous glow, and her womb conceived. Twelve years went by. On the fourth day of the tenth moon at midnight, Fu-Xi was born, thus named in memory of the river on whose bank he was conceived."*

Among the ancient Mexicans, Christ is Quetzalcoatl, who was the Messiah and transformer of the Toltecs.

> *"One day, while Chimalman was alone with her two sisters, a messenger from heaven appeared before her. On seeing him, the sisters died of fright. Chimalman*

> *heard from the mouth of the angel that she*
> *would conceive a son, and she instantly*
> *conceived Quetzalcoatl, without the help of*
> *a male."*

Quetzalcoatl was the Messiah of the Toltecs.

Among the Japanese, Christ is Amida, who intercedes before the Supreme Goddess Tenshokodaijin ["Heaven-shining-mighty goddess"], praying for all sinners. Amida is the Japanese Christ of the Shinto religion, and is the one who has the power to open the doors of Tenju-koku (paradise).

The German Eddas mention "Kristos," the God of their theogony. who like Jesus of Nazareth, was born at Christmas, the 25th of December at midnight, just like the Christified Nordics, Odin, Wotan, and Belen.

Krishna's gospel in millenary India is similar to the Christian gospel. The birth of Krishna is similar to the birth of Jesus. By the work and Grace of the Holy Spirit, Devaki conceived Krishna. The Child God Krishna was transported to the stable of the shepherds, the stable of Nanden, and the gods and angels came to adore him.

Among the Greeks, Christ is Zeus, and among the Romans, he is thundering Jupiter.

The Kristos Jupiter, Zeus, Apollo, are born from immaculate virgins.

In old Egypt of the Pharaohs, Christ is Osiris, and all those who incarnated him were Osirified.

Hermes Trismegistus is the Egyptian Christ, who incarnated Osiris (Christ). Every man who succeeds in assimilating the Christ substance is in fact converted into a living Christ.

The Virgin Mother of the Christified

The Virgin Mother of the Christified beings is the Divine Mother Kundalini, the Cosmic Mother, God the Mother, universal, infinite love, which is co-essential with the Absolute Abstract Space, Isis, Mary, Rhea, Tonantzin, etc.

The Manger of the World

The stable or manger where the Child God is born is the divine dwelling of the soul, the eternal temple now invaded by the animals of desire. It is urgent to know that unfortunately, within the kingdom of the soul, there are animal elementaries of desire. They nourish themselves with the inferior substances of the lower animal depths of man. There live and multiply all those animal elementaries that constitute what is called ego; therefore, it is not an exaggeration to say that the I exists in a pluralized form. The I is constituted by animal elementaries, the animals of the stable where the Child God is born to save man.

Each animal elementary represents a specific defect; whenever we annihilate a defect, its corresponding elementary dies. We need to die from instant to instant. We need to dissolve the psychological I that always reincarnates to satisfy desires.

The New Aquarian Age

Much has been said about the new age of Aquarius that will begin the 4th of February, 1962, between two and three in the afternoon. Some assume that the new age has already begun, but this assumption is false; the new era will begin on the 4th of February, 1962.

The seven ruling genii of the seven planets—the Moon, Mercury, the Sun, Mars, Jupiter, Venus, and Saturn—shall meet at a cosmic congress at the aforementioned hour. There will be an eclipse of the sun and moon at that hour, visible in some places of the Old World. This event will be a sort of congregation of celestial traffic in the constellation of Aquarius. Thus, the new era shall begin with that event. The concrete cosmic facts are what speak; the cosmic event of the 4th of February, 1962, is only repeated every two thousand, one hundred and sixty years, in a particular constellation, each time that a new era begins.

Thus, 1962 will be the first year of Aquarius. All the brothers of the Gnostic Movement should date their letters according to the new era. The cosmic event of 1962 will initiate many catastrophes in different parts of the world.

Planetary congress on February 4th, 1962 that occurred under the influence of the constellation of Aquarius, which marked the beginning of the new era.

The Age of Pisces

The age of Pisces that ends on the 4th of February, 1962, was the age of dogmatic Christianity struggling against atheist materialism. If we observe the sign of Pisces, we see two fish, duality, the struggle between two opposing ideologies: spiritualism and materialism in total battle, the church and the state at war, science and religion in conflict.

The fish that lives under the waters and is carried by the currents is instinctive and brutal, like the people of the Piscean age. The man of that era does not know how to handle nor transmute the waters of life, in other words, the seminal liquor.

The Age of Aquarius

The Aquarian age that will begin on the 4th of February, 1962, is the age of synthesis.

In the sign of Pisces, the human being does not know how to handle the seminal liquor, the waters of life. In the sign of Aquarius, a man appears with two pitchers of water, wisely combining the waters at will and with wisdom.

In the new Aquarian age, the human being will adopt the synthesis of all religions. This synthesis is Sexual Magic, and the Christ in substance.

In the Aquarian age, man will know how to transmute the seminal liquor.

In the Aquarian age, man will accomplish marvels in the fields of endocrinology, atomic physics, chemistry, astronomy, astrology, medicine, aviation, etc.

The Doctrine of the Synthesis

The Gnostic Movement teaches the doctrine of the synthesis, which is contained in the substance in all the religions of the world. Sexual Magic is practiced in Zen Buddhism. Sexual Magic is practiced among the Sufis. Sexual Magic is practiced in secret Christianity. Sexual Magic was practiced in the mystery schools of Mexico, the highlands of Peru, Egypt, Greece, Persia, India, etc.

The dissolution of the I is studied and taught in Zen Buddhism, Christianity, and generally in all the great religions. This is the path of sanctity.

The Buddhists of Zen say that the dissolution of the I is Nirvana. The Christian

mystics aspire to die in the Lord. All
the religions want sanctity to die in the
Lord—in other words, to dissolve the I.

The doctrine of the new Aquarian age is
the doctrine of the synthesis. The doctrine
that the Gnostic Movement teaches is
the doctrine of the synthesis. We are not
against any religion, school, or system of
spiritual teaching. We teach the synthesis
of all the religions and systems of the realization of the Inner Self. That is all.

The synthesis does not result from
mixtures. The synthesis exists as a fact,
without contrived mixtures. The synthesis
is the perfect marriage and the dissolution of the I. God shines upon the perfect
couple.

Wherever is found a marriage practic-
ing Sexual Magic and working in the dissolution of the I, the Synthesis is there.

Let us remember that religion has a
sexual origin. Let us remember that man
exists because of sex, and that the origin
of all life is sexual.

Prophecies for the Future

The Christ in substance, the perfect
matrimony, and sanctity constitute the

perfect synthesis of all the religions of the world.

When all the religions of the world have disappeared, the cosmic Christ and sanctity—the synthesis that is indestructible, and the eternal of all eternity—will continue to exist.

In the Aquarian age, the dogmatic type of Christianity will no longer be taught. In Aquarius, all dogmatic forms will disappear. In the New Era, Christ will be comprehended as a substance.

In the new Aquarian age, everything will be atomic and explosive. People will then be prepared to study the doctrine of the synthesis. Science will be religious, and religion will be scientific. Arguments related to the subjects of the spirit and matter will disappear, and people will comprehend that both spirit and matter are modifications of the universal energy.

In the Aquarian age, devices will be invented to see egos that have disembodied.

There shall be a collision of magnetic fields of worlds. Our Earth's magnetic field will collide with that of another planet. This event will put an end to the present Aryan race.

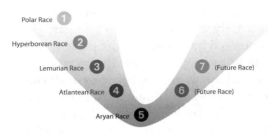

The Seven Root Races of the Terrestrial Cosmic Era

The entire Earth will then go through a total and definite transformation. The selected, the chosen, will be secretly saved, and they shall serve as seeds for the sixth race.

This collision of magnetic fields of worlds is not new. In archaic times, the Earth had a similar collision. At that time, our Earth was closer to the Sun, and was flung by the collision to the place it occupies now.

The age that is about to begin will be governed by Aquarius. This sign governs the Earth's atmosphere. Aquarius is in the house of Uranus, which we know is atomic and explosive. Therefore, what will happen is approaching our atmosphere and is explosive.

The Earth and all its elements will burn intensely with fire. The ancient Earth was destroyed by water, and the present Earth will be destroyed by fire. In this manner, all the written prophecies in all the sacred books of all religions, of east and west, of north and south, will be fulfilled. The word of all those who incarnated the Cosmic Christ will be totally fulfilled.

In the Aquarian age, atomic wars fought to death will take place. The Third World War will be a fact. The result of all these wars will be terrible: horrible earthquakes, seaquakes, unknown illnesses, hunger, misery, etc.

Very soon, man will conquer the Moon. It is necessary to know that man will reach other planets with his rockets. It is urgent to comprehend that when the man of Aquarius manages to arm a powerful fleet of cosmic ships to violently invade other planets in space, then on that day shall be fulfilled all the prophecies of those who incarnated the Cosmic Christ in substance. That shall be the day of the collision of worlds, the mountains made dust will fly through the air, and all that has life shall perish by fire.

The men of the future Earth, the men of the future great race, the men of the sixth race that will appear after the great cataclysm, will have to begin their lives in the caverns of the transformed Earth of this modern civilization, for everything will be destroyed. When everything has been destroyed, when the Aryan race has disappeared, only the doctrine of the synthesis shall continue to exist.

"The Age of Aquarius"

Much has been said about the Aquarian age. Some are awaiting it, others assume that it began a long time ago. We go by the facts. On the 4th of February of 1962, between two and three o'clock in the afternoon, astronomers throughout the entire world will witness something unusual. All the planets of that time will go through a conjunction of worlds. All the planets of our solar system will assemble in council under the constellation of Aquarius. Such an event only happens when a new era will follow. Therefore, facts are facts, and we must surrender before the facts.

We are not making utopian affirmations. What we emphasize has been duly verified by all astronomical observatories.

Therefore, it is obvious that on the aforementioned date the age of Aquarius will really be initiated, amidst the august thunder of thought.

Many predict a "Golden Age" after the year 2000. They believe that the Aquarian age, with all its splendor and beauty, is certain to manifest itself fully after the year 2000. It is predicted that this humanity shall undergo a radical transformation after the year 2000. Obviously my dear brothers and sisters, such "prophecies" fail. They are no more than sophisms. And, what is a sophism? A sophism is a thick wall without a foundation; a light push is enough to convert it into small bits of sediment.

Unquestionably, it is not possible for the psychological "I" of the multitudes to create a Golden Age. It is absurd to suppose that the collective ego could originate an age of light and beauty.

Within us are the factors of discord that produce wars, egoism, hatred, violence, lust. When egoism and violence express themselves collectively, war appears on the stage of life. Do you believe that in these circumstances the ego could create an age of fraternity and love?

With what laborers are we going to build the edifice of the Aquarian age? Which multitudes are capable of establishing an era of splendor and love on the face of the Earth?

You who know people very well, that talk with your fellowmen, that know what a struggle it is to earn your daily bread, that know what envy is, who have suffered and caused others to suffer, could you accept the thesis that such people with whom you live are capable of initiating an age of beauty and splendor? It is said that a tree is known by its fruits.

Therefore, reflecting, sincerely and wholeheartedly, those who predict an age of beauty and splendors after the year 2,000 are mistaken.

In order to create, it is necessary to destroy. On arriving at this part, diverse theosophical and astrological concepts, etc. come to my memory.

Many are the various theorists who conceptualize that a revolution of the earth's axes will be necessary, and that

before the age of light, said revolution
will be produced. They say that the waters
shall invade part of the Earth—not the
entire Earth—and that millions shall perish by water.

They suppose that a portion of the
Earth will be flung into space to become a
new moon. They believe that this portion
will be separated from the austral region,
and will form a new satellite around our
Earth. Next, they say, will come the era of
splendors.

These are very beautiful concepts, and
very tragic as well, but very erroneous. All
those who suppose that the future cataclysms will be by water are wrong, because
if we accept that thesis, we would have to
burn the Second Epistle of Peter to the
Romans and the gospel of Jesus, especially
that page of the prophetic sermon. There
are details you can see in the second
Epistle of Peter to the Romans that the
destruction that now awaits us will be by
fire. Peter already said that the ancient
era was destroyed by water. He also said
that today's Earth shall be destroyed by
fire, that all elements will be destroyed
as they burn, and that all the works that
are in them will be burnt. Therefore,

whoever has faith that the next cataclysm will be by water is mistaken. That would be a repetition of the Atlantean tragedy. Then, what the prophets said would be undoubtedly destroyed. But, it is not so.

Obviously, the words of Peter will be fulfilled, and what Mohammed said will also be fulfilled, and what all the prophets said will also be fulfilled.

The catastrophe that awaits our world shall be by fire. The Aztecs said that the sons of the fifth sun would perish by fire and earthquakes, and the prophecy has already begun to be fulfilled.

We know very well that at the bottom of the Atlantic and the Pacific there are very deep cracks, and that some are so deep that they allow the contact of the water with the fire from the interior of the earth. The result is that pressures and vapors are increasing from instant to instant. Consequently, the Earth trembles everywhere. These pressures and vapors will intensify so that earthquakes will propagate worldwide. Therefore, that is the crude, factual reality that awaits us in Aquarius.

Theologians do not know how to interpret this matter. They say, "Aquarius is the sign of science, a sign of air, that shall conquer the infinite space, where frontiers shall end, and all will be love." Just like that, because Aquarius arrives, the entire world will transform itself? Without working? Without making any effort at all? In other words, mechanically, the one who is evil will stop being evil and become a "soul of God"? According to them, he will never be evil again, as if one could transform oneself mechanically, as if one did not have to struggle within to transform himself, to put an end to his psychological defects. To think such a thing is absurd.

After the constellation of Aquarius comes Leo, which is the constellation of love, the one that gives the scepters to kings and creates fraternity. All this is very fine, but if they knew the crude reality of things, they would know that Leo is none other than the constellation of fire. What does this mean? That all this will be consumed by fire. The lion will finish it all. The Lion of the Law will not leave anything alive, and all this will be converted into ashes. Nothing of this great Babylon will be left.

Beloved,

I wish thee a happy Christmas. May the star of Bethlehem shine on thy path. May thy Father who is in Secret and thy divine and adorable Mother Kundalini bless thy own Being.

Samael Aun Weor

Glossary

Chastity: "virtuous, pure from unlawful sexual intercourse," from O.Fr. chaste "morally pure," from L. castus "pure, chaste." Although modern usage has rendered the term chastity virtually meaningless to most people, its original meaning and usage clearly indicate "moral purity" upon the basis of "sexual purity." Contemporary usage implies "repression" or "abstinence," which have nothing to do with real chastity. True chastity is a rejection of impure sexuality. True chastity is pure sexuality, or the activity of sex in harmony with our true nature, as explained in the secret doctrine. Properly used, the word chastity refers to sexual fidelity or honor.

"The generative energy, which, when we are loose, dissipates and makes us unclean, when we are continent invigorates and inspires us. Chastity is the flowering of man; and what are called Genius, Heroism, Holiness, and the like, are but various fruits which succeed it." - Henry David Thoreau, *Walden*

"On me may chastity, heaven's fairest gift, look with a favouring eye; never may Cypris, goddess dread, fasten on me a temper to dispute, or restless jealousy, smiting my soul with mad desire for unlawful love, but may she hallow peaceful married life and shrewdly decide whom each of us shall wed." - *Medea* by Euripides

"Be sober, diligent, and chaste; avoid all wrath.
In public or in secret ne'er permit thou any evil;
and above all else respect thyself." - Pythagoras

"The man who by chastity preserves himself
pure, fears no judgment for he is united with
the name of the Holy One." - The Zohar

Christ: Derived from the Greek Christos, "the
Anointed One," and Krestos, whose esoteric
meaning is "fire." The word Christ is a title, not
a personal name.

"Indeed, Christ is a Sephirothic Crown (Kether,
Chokmah and Binah) of incommensurable
wisdom, whose purest atoms shine within
Chokmah, the world of the Ophanim. Christ is
not the Monad, Christ is not the Theosophical
Septenary; Christ is not the Jivan-Atman. Christ
is the Central Sun. Christ is the ray that unites
us to the Absolute." - Samael Aun Weor, *Tarot
and Kabbalah*

"The Gnostic Church adores the Saviour of the
World, Jesus. The Gnostic Church knows that
Jesus incarnated Christ, and that is why they
adore him. Christ is not a human nor a divine
individual. Christ is a title given to all fully
self-realised Masters. Christ is the Army of the
Voice. Christ is the Verb. The Verb is far beyond
the body, the soul and the Spirit. Everyone who
is able to incarnate the Verb receives in fact
the title of Christ. Christ is the Verb itself. It is
necessary for everyone of us to incarnate the
Verb (Word). When the Verb becomes flesh in
us we speak with the verb of light. In actuality,
several Masters have incarnated the Christ. In
secret India, the Christ Yogi Babaji has lived for

millions of years; Babaji is immortal. The Great
Master of Wisdom Kout Humi also incarnated
the Christ. Sanat Kumara, the founder of the
Great College of Initiates of the White Lodge,
is another living Christ. In the past, many
incarnated the Christ. In the present, some
have incarnated the Christ. In the future many
will incarnate the Christ. John the Baptist also
incarnated the Christ. John the Baptist is a living Christ. The difference between Jesus and the
other Masters that also incarnated the Christ
has to do with Hierarchy. Jesus is the highest
Solar Initiate of the Cosmos..." - Samael Aun
Weor, *The Perfect Matrimony*

Consciousness: "Wherever there is life, there exists
the consciousness. Consciousness is inherent to
life as humidity is inherent to water." - Samael
Aun Weor, *Fundamental Notions of Endocrinology
and Criminology*

From various dictionaries: 1. The state of being
conscious; knowledge of one's own existence,
condition, sensations, mental operations, acts,
etc. 2. Immediate knowledge or perception of
the presence of any object, state, or sensation. 3.
An alert cognitive state in which you are aware
of yourself and your situation. In Universal
Gnosticism, the range of potential consciousness is allegorized in the Ladder of Jacob, upon
which the angels ascend and descend. Thus
there are higher and lower levels of consciousness, from the level of demons at the bottom, to
highly realized angels in the heights.

"It is vital to understand and develop the con-
viction that consciousness has the potential to

increase to an infinite degree." - The 14th Dalai Lama

"Light and consciousness are two phenomena of the same thing; to a lesser degree of consciousness, corresponds a lesser degree of light; to a greater degree of consciousness, a greater degree of light." - Samael Aun Weor, *The Esoteric Treatise of Hermetic Astrology*

Divine Mother: "Among the Aztecs, she was known as Tonantzin, among the Greeks as chaste Diana. In Egypt she was Isis, the Divine Mother, whose veil no mortal has lifted. There is no doubt at all that esoteric Christianity has never forsaken the worship of the Divine Mother Kundalini. Obviously she is Marah, or better said, RAM-IO, MARY. What orthodox religions did not specify, at least with regard to the exoteric or public circle, is the aspect of Isis in her individual human form. Clearly, it was taught only in secret to the Initiates that this Divine Mother exists individually within each human being. It cannot be emphasized enough that Mother-God, Rhea, Cybele, Adonia, or whatever we wish to call her, is a variant of our own individual Being in the here and now. Stated explicitly, each of us has our own particular, individual Divine Mother." - Samael Aun Weor, *The Great Rebellion*

"Devi Kundalini, the Consecrated Queen of Shiva, our personal Divine Cosmic Individual Mother, assumes five transcendental mystic aspects in every creature, which we must enumerate:

1. The unmanifested Prakriti

2. The chaste Diana, Isis, Tonantzin, Maria or better said Ram-Io

3. The terrible Hecate, Persephone, Coatlicue, queen of the infernos and death; terror of love and law

4. The special individual Mother Nature, creator and architect of our physical organism

5. The Elemental Enchantress to whom we owe every vital impulse, every instinct." - Samael Aun Weor, *The Mystery of the Golden Blossom*

Ego: The multiplicity of contradictory psychological elements that we have inside are in their sum the "ego." Each one is also called "an ego" or an "I." Every ego is a psychological defect which produces suffering. The ego is three (related to our Three Brains or three centers of psychological processing), seven (capital sins), and legion (in their infinite variations).

"The ego is the root of ignorance and pain." - Samael Aun Weor, *The Esoteric Treatise of Hermetic Astrology*

"The Being and the ego are incompatible. The Being and the ego are like water and oil. They can never be mixed... The annihilation of the psychic aggregates (egos) can be made possible only by radically comprehending our errors through meditation and by the evident Self-reflection of the Being." - Samael Aun Weor, *The Gnostic Bible: The Pistis Sophia Unveiled*

Fornication: Originally, the term fornication was derived from the Indo-European word gwher, whose meanings relate to heat and burning (the full explanation can be found online at

http://sacred-sex.org/terminology/fornication).
Fornication means to make the heat (solar
fire) of the seed (sexual power) leave the body
through voluntary orgasm. Any voluntary
orgasm is fornication, whether between a married man and woman, or an unmarried man
and woman, or through masturbation, or in
any other case; this is explained by Moses: "A
man from whom there is a discharge of semen,
shall immerse all his flesh in water, and he shall
remain unclean until evening. And any garment
or any leather [object] which has semen on it,
shall be immersed in water, and shall remain
unclean until evening. A woman with whom a
man cohabits, whereby there was [a discharge
of] semen, they shall immerse in water, and they
shall remain unclean until evening." - Leviticus
15:16-18

To fornicate is to spill the sexual energy
through the orgasm. Those who "deny themselves" restrain the sexual energy, and "walk in
the midst of the fire" without being burned.
Those who restrain the sexual energy, who
renounce the orgasm, remember God in themselves, and do not defile themselves with animal
passion, "for the temple of God is holy, which
temple ye are."

"Whosoever is born of God doth not commit
sin; for his seed remaineth in him: and he cannot sin, because he is born of God." - 1 John 3:9

This is why neophytes always took a vow of
sexual abstention, so that they could prepare
themselves for marriage, in which they would
have sexual relations but not release the sexual

energy through the orgasm. This is why Paul advised:

"...they that have wives be as though they had none..." - I Corinthians 7:29

"A fornicator is an individual who has intensely accustomed his genital organs to copulate (with orgasm). Yet, if the same individual changes his custom of copulation to the custom of no copulation, then he transforms himself into a chaste person. We have as an example the astonishing case of Mary Magdalene, who was a famous prostitute. Mary Magdalene became the famous Saint Mary Magdalene, the repented prostitute. Mary Magdalene became the chaste disciple of Christ." - Samael Aun Weor, *The Revolution of Beelzebub*

Gnosis: (Greek) Knowledge.

1. The word Gnosis refers to the knowledge we acquire through our own experience, as opposed to knowledge that we are told or believe in. Gnosis - by whatever name in history or culture - is conscious, experiential knowledge, not merely intellectual or conceptual knowledge, belief, or theory. This term is synonymous with the Hebrew "daath" and the Sanskrit "jna."

2. The tradition that embodies the core wisdom or knowledge of humanity.

"Gnosis is the flame from which all religions sprouted, because in its depth Gnosis is religion. The word "religion" comes from the Latin word "religare," which implies "to link the Soul to God"; so Gnosis is the very pure flame from where all religions sprout, because Gnosis is

Knowledge, Gnosis is Wisdom." - Samael Aun Weor, The Esoteric Path

"The secret science of the Sufis and of the Whirling Dervishes is within Gnosis. The secret doctrine of Buddhism and of Taoism is within Gnosis. The sacred magic of the Nordics is within Gnosis. The wisdom of Hermes, Buddha, Confucius, Mohammed and Quetzalcoatl, etc., etc., is within Gnosis. Gnosis is the Doctrine of Christ." - Samael Aun Weor, The Revolution of Beelzebub

Holy Spirit: The Christian name for the third aspect of the Holy Trinity, or "God." This force has other names in other religions. In Kabbalah, the third sephirah, Binah. In Buddhism, it is related to Nirmanakaya, the "body of formation" through which the inner Buddha works in the world.

"The Holy Spirit is the Fire of Pentecost or the fire of the Holy Spirit called Kundalini by the Hindus, the igneous serpent of our magical powers, Holy Fire symbolized by Gold..." - Samael Aun Weor, The Perfect Matrimony

"It has been said in The Divine Comedy with complete clarity that the Holy Spirit is the husband of the Divine Mother. Therefore, the Holy Spirit unfolds himself into his wife, into the Shakti of the Hindus. This must be known and understood. Some, when they see that the Third Logos is unfolded into the Divine Mother Kundalini, or Shakti, She that has many names, have believed that the Holy Spirit is feminine, and they have been mistaken. The Holy Spirit is masculine, but when He unfolds Himself into

She, then the first ineffable Divine Couple is formed, the Creator Elohim, the Kabir, or Great Priest, the Ruach Elohim, that in accordance to Moses, cultivated the waters in the beginning of the world." - Samael Aun Weor, *Tarot and Kabbalah*

"The Primitive Gnostic Christians worshipped the lamb, the fish and the white dove as symbols of the Holy Spirit." - Samael Aun Weor, *The Perfect Matrimony*

Jesus: The central personage of Christianity is called Jesus Christ, but this is not his birth name, it is an acquired title. The name "Jesus" is derived from an Aramaic (ancient Hebrew) word, Yeshua, which means "savior." Thus, the original use of this term is as an honorific title, such as "rabbi."

Vestal: A term derived from Roman religion, referring to a priestess of Vesta. The term refers to a sacred duty performed by virginal (sexually pure) women in many esoteric traditions. In Roman times, while still little girls, they were chosen from prominent Roman families. Their duties included the preparation of sacrifices and the tending of the sacred fire. If any vestal broke her vow of chastity, it is said that she was entombed alive. The vestals had great influence in the Roman state.

"The woman is the vestal of the temple; thus, the fire of the temple is lit by the vestal. In ancient times, the fire was guarded and lit by the vestals. This symbolizes that only the woman has the unique capability of lighting her husband's fire of Kundalini, which is the fire from our body or our temple. The temple of the very high, living God is our body and the fire of this temple is the Kundalini, which our vestal-spouse lights by means of the same sexual contact, or Sexual Magic, as taught in the book The Perfect Matrimony or the Door to Enter into Initiation, and as well within this current book. In this present time, the Roman Catholic Church has totally lost this tradition. That is why we see that in this Roman Church the fire of the temple is lit by acolyte boys, an action that is not only an absurdity, but moreover, a very grave sacrilege and an insult to life itself." - Samael Aun Weor, The Revolution of Beelzebub

"In that [past] epoch, there were sacred priestesses inside the temples, special Vestals. The celibate male initiates worked with these Vestals. In this day and age such women inside of the Lumisials would not be beneficial... They would be scandalous. Therefore, in this day and age, the Maithuna, Sex Yoga, can only and must only be practiced between husband and wife, within legitimate, constituted marriages." - Samael Aun Weor, The Gnostic Magic of the Runes

Virgin: (1) A state of sexual purity; or (2) an esoteric degree of initiation.

"Religious people know that a Virgin named "Immaculate Conception" exists. Any mystic-illuminati perfectly knows that she lives in Eden working with the immaculate conceptions of the Holy Spirit. When a conception without the spilling of the seminal fluid is performed, it is done by the Holy Spirit. Such a conception is under the vigilance and direction of the "Immaculate Conception." We announce that this said Virgin is not the Hebrew Mary. Indeed, the "Immaculate Conception" is a woman who attained the degree of Virgin. Many similar women exist, true living Buddhas who attained the Fifth Initiation. Let us remember the Virgin of the Sea (Mother of Jesus), and the eleven thousand Inca Virgins, the Virgins of the stars, the Virgin of the law, etc. All of those women are living Buddhas, women who attained the Fifth Initiation of Major Mysteries (true human beings). The most elevated degree for a woman is that of Virgin. The most elevated degree for a human is that of Christ. The Virgin who renounces Nirvana and reincarnates in order to work for humanity as a human being elevates herself to the degree of Christ." - Samael Aun Weor, *Aztec Christic Magic*

About the Author

The name Samael Aun Weor is Hebrew and is pronounced "sam-ayel on vay-ohr."

Between 1950 and 1977—merely twenty-seven years—Samael Aun Weor wrote over seventy books and established the international Gnostic Movement across the entire span of Latin America: stretching across twenty countries and an area of more than 21,000,000 kilometers, with Gnostic schools everywhere, even in places where there are no electricity, paved roads, or post offices.

During those twenty-seven years, he experienced all the extremes that humanity could give him, from adoration to death threats, and in spite of the enormous popularity of his books and lectures, he renounced an income, refused recognitions, walked away from accolades, and consistently turned away those who would worship him. He held as friends both presidents and peasants, and yet remained a mystery to all.

When one reflects on the effort and will it requires to perform even day to day tasks, it is astonishing to consider the herculean efforts required to accomplish what he did in such a short time. But, there is a reason: he was a man who knew who he was, and what he had to do. Yet, in spite of his wisdom and generosity towards mankind, he said: "Do not follow me. I am just a signpost. Reach your own Self-realization." His lifelong mission was to deliver to humanity the total and exact science to develop the complete human being, that mysterious and ancient wisdom long hidden in the bosom of every great religion. You can learn more about him at SamaelAunWeor.info

Index

Glorian Publishing is a non-profit publisher dedicated to spreading the sacred universal doctrine to suffering humanity. All of our works are made possible by the kindness and generosity of sponsors. If you would like to make a tax-deductible donation, you may send it to the address below, or visit our website for other alternatives. If you would like to sponsor the publication of a book, please contact us at 877-726-2359 or help@gnosticteachings.org.

Glorian Publishing
PO Box 110225
Brooklyn, NY 11211 US
Phone: 877-726-2359

VISIT US ONLINE AT:

gnosticteachings.org